AZU's Dreams of Singapore
Singapore
Published in 2006 by AZU Editions Ltd.
13/F, Silver Fortune Plaza
1 Wellington Street
Central, Hong Kong
www.azueditions.com

Produced by ink it Group Co. Ltd.
111 SKV Building, 3/F
Soi Sansabai, Sukhumvit Soi 36
Klongton, Klongtoey
Bangkok 10110, Thailand
Tel: 66 (0) 2661 2893
Fax: 66 (0) 2661 2895
info@inkitgroup.com
www.inkitgroup.com

ISBN 988-98581-3-4

Printed in Malaysia

Copyright 2006 AZU Editions Ltd.

All rights reserved. No part of this publication may be reproduced, stored in a retrieval system or transmitted in any form by any means, electronic, mechanical, photocopying, recording or otherwise, without the prior written permission of AZU Editions Ltd. All content, text, illustrations and photographs in this publication are protected by national and international trademark and copyright laws. Any infringement of the rights of AZU Editions Ltd. may lead to prosecution without warning.

For information about reproduction rights to the photographs in this book, contact ink it Group Co. Ltd.

Cover: The glittering Esplanade – Theatres on the Bay is the centrepiece of Singapore's vibrant cultural scene.

Sponsored by

Singapore Tourism Board

SINGAPORE — A CITY LIKE NO OTHER,
A WORLD OF POSSIBILITIES

visitsingapore.com

AZU'S
DREAMS OF SINGAPORE™

Singapore

Photographs by Joakim Leroy
Text by Michael Spencer

AZU

Glistening
like a tropical jewel

at the southernmost tip of the Malay peninsula, Singapore is a strikingly modern city where futuristic architecture blends effortlessly with antique colonial buildings and quaint shophouses. One of the greenest and cleanest of all Asian capitals, it is a place where landscape gardening and urban planning has been raised to a high art form to the delight of its residents and visitors alike.

Legend has it that its name derives from a 14th-century incident when a prince of Johor

Previous spread: *A panoramic view of the Central Business District.*

Left: *Boat Quay swings at night.*

spied a lion on the shore of the island and founded a settlement there called *Singapura*, or 'lion city'. It was no more than a tiny fishing village when it was awoken from obscurity in January 1819 by the arrival of Sir Thomas Stamford Raffles, then British governor of Sumatra. He had chosen this unlikely spot to be the site of a new free-trade port and its destiny was to change dramatically as a result.

With a strategic location at the epicentre of the sea routes between Europe and China, Singapore soon developed into the most important trading centre in Southeast Asia. From its earliest days merchants, traders and adventurers flocked here from far and wide, populating the city with a rich tapestry

Above left: *Sir Thomas Stamford Raffles, the founder of Singapore.*

Right: *British colonial buildings like the Central Fire Station are built in the Moorish style.*

of cultures, religions and races. Although most are of Chinese origin, the population is an ethnic mosaic that includes Malay, Arab, Indian and Eurasian elements.

This spicy cultural mix has given Singapore a rich personality that becomes more layered and nuanced the more closely it is examined. Much of the city is still a fascinating patchwork of temples, restaurants and shophouses reflecting the origins of its inhabitants whether they are Hokkien, Cantonese, Tamil, Bugis or Punjabi.

Even 'Singlish', the unofficial but widely spoken English patois, is a reflection of this cultural melting pot, incorporating words and grammar from various Chinese dialects as well as Malay and Indian languages. All this begs the question, what is it that binds these diverse people together? Singaporeans themselves have come to the conclusion that their unifying cultural thread is simply food, glorious food. Eating is widely recognized as the national pastime, and the ubiquitous hawker centres that serve a bewildering selection of delicacies from all over Asia are where Singaporeans of all backgrounds come together in harmony and delight.

Singapore has capitalized on its assets of great food and fabulous shopping to become a major Asian tourist destination. The main boulevard, Orchard Road, is lined with high-end shopping malls packed with designer boutiques and slinky department stores. Fun innovations like Night Safari at the Singapore Zoo and the theme park

Above left:
A vibrant street market in Little India.

Right:
Singaporeans beat the heat with cool desserts like ice kachang.

attractions on Sentosa Island are so popular they have been widely copied elsewhere.

Keen to keep its unique character alive, historic buildings in Singapore are refurbished and put to new uses. The grand colonial post office has been transformed into a stunning hotel, and on Boat Quay rows of Art Deco shophouses have found fresh life as trendy restaurants and bars. In contrast to the gleaming towers of the Central Business District, parts of Little India and Chinatown have managed to retain their old-world charm. A stroll through their narrow streets can reveal scenes that seem hardly to have changed since Joseph Conrad immortalized exotic 19th-century Singapore as the quintessential tropical port in his novels.

Above left: Renovated shophouses have now become desirable residences.

Right: Trishaws are the perfect way to explore Serangoon Road in Little India.

Left: The futuristic Esplanade – Theatres on the Bay is the centrepiece of art and culture.

Following spread: Suntec Singapore and Suntec city are an integrated office, shopping and convention centre.

Singapore is not just preserving the past but adding thought-provoking new elements like the Esplanade – Theatres on the Bay to the mix. Adding weight to Singapore's bid to promote itself as a centre for arts and culture, the Esplanade is also a centrepiece for the annual Singapore Arts Festival that is gaining worldwide recognition as a premier showcase of music, theatre and dance.

If Raffles was Singapore's founder, the man who has shaped its modern destiny is Lee Kuan Yew. During his 30 years as Prime Minister, he laid the foundations for what Singapore has become today: a superbly planned and executed urban marvel that is also endlessly fascinating and lots of fun!

Previous pages (left):
Statue of a sacred cow at the Hindu Sri Mariamman Temple. ***(right):*** Lovingly restored 19th-century shophouses.

Left: Raffles Hotel, an international icon of opulence and hospitality.

Above: Traditionally, doormen at the Raffles Hotel are impressive Sikhs.

Above: *The clock tower at the cricket club, a vestige of the British Empire.*

Right: *The imposing domed old Supreme Court building stands across the road from the Padang, Singapore's green heart.*

Above: *Arab Street, bursting with stalls and shops selling an eclectic and exotic mix of goods, is easy to explore on foot.*

Right: *Chinatown shophouses contrast with the modern skyscrapers of the Central Business District.*

Above: Singapore girls are famously fashion-conscious.

Right: Tree-lined Orchard Road is a mecca for shoppers.

Above: *Descended from the rickshaw, trishaws are a fun way to travel around.*

Right: *Raffles Place, in the heart of the Central Business District.*

Left: *Shopping malls such as Raffles City are a great Singaporean institution.* **Above:** *Another satisfied customer for luxury goods departs an upscale mall.*

Following spread: *Clarke Quay draws revellers to its many bars, restaurants and entertainment establishments.*

Above: Take a relaxing bumboat ride along the Singapore River. *Right:* An effortless blend of the old and the new at Boat Quay.

Following spread: Tree-lined roads are a pleasing and common feature of the Singapore landscape.

Left: *Mount Faber offers a great view of the busy sea lanes.*

Above: *Dockers at PSA Singapore Terminals, the world's largest container transhipment hub.*

Above: *A bulbul rests on a park bench.*

Right: *A refreshing stroll in the Singapore Botanic Gardens.*

Left: The imposing Sultan Mosque dominates Arab Street. *Above:* The Malay community keeps its traditions alive.

Following pages: Many of Singapore's prominent Hindu community worship at the Sri Mariamman Temple.

Above: *Traditional Chinese arts like calligraphy still flourish.* ***Right:*** *In Chinatown the street stalls are a great attraction.*

Following pages: *Buddhism is a major religion among the Chinese community in Singapore.*

Above: *Sentosa island.*

Right: *Singapore's beach playground.*

Following pages (left): *No.5 Emerald Hill Cocktail Bar, one of the chic bars in a converted shophouse on Emerald Hill.* ***(right):*** *Young Singaporeans party until dawn at Ministry of Sound on Clarke Quay.* ***(spread):*** *Sunset on Marina Bay.*

UNIQUELY Singapore

'What is unique about Singapore? I think it's the people, very warm, loving and caring.'
Abhishek Bachchan, Bollywood actor

Unique is the word that best captures Singapore. A city like no other, it is an ever-changing mosaic of fascinating contrasts. Of East and West. Of rich legacies and sleek modern living. Of ancient beliefs and contemporary culture. And of experiences so uniquely enchanting and enriching, it's beyond words.

Left:
Multi-ethnic kids play under the watchful gaze of Sir Thomas Stamford Raffles.

Left: Taste a variety of local delights on Chinatown Food Street. (inset): Drinking and dining al fresco is an activity visitors will enjoy.

Above right: Get your adrenaline pumping with a reverse bungee jump.

Only in Singapore can you . . .

- Feast around the clock and savour mouth-watering dishes not found anywhere else, with settings ranging from a cable car to a riverboat along the Singapore River . . .

- Get your hands on the latest buys from luxury labels or shop for basement bargains at four in the morning . . .

- Have breakfast with an orangutan, learn about the Chinese tea ceremony and watch a Broadway musical all in one day . . .

- Get catapulted 60 metres into the air on a reverse bungee jump or board an amphibious 'duck' to explore the city . . .

- Dive with sharks, get up close and personal with cheetahs or enjoy a high-tea buffet 70 storeys in the air . . .

- Luxuriate in a garden spa a stone's throw from the best business facilities in the world . . .

- Visit a Chinese temple, Muslim mosque, Hindu temple and Christian church all in one neighbourhood . . .

- Mingle with local youths along Orchard Road, and pick up the latest fashion tips and amusing local catchphrases . . .

- Check out orchids named after well-known personalities such as Nelson Mandela, Princess Diana and Bae Yong-Jun.

Above left: Visit the National Orchid Garden and see over 1,000 orchid species and hybrids.

Right: Orchard Road buzzes with shoppers day and night. *(inset):* The dizzying towers of the Central Financial District.

Left: Ice kachang *is Singapore's favourite and most colourful dessert.* *(inset):* Roti prata *is a popular breakfast snack that originates from India.*

Right: Stop by the shops and wet market in Little India for an array of fruits, vegetables and spices.

- Choose from 30 different *prata*s, ranging from cheese *prata* to a chocolate one or even a *prata* accompanied by a scoop of your favourite ice-cream flavour.

Singapore – a city like no other, a world of possibilities.

'Food-crazed Singapore is probably the best place on earth for sampling the astonishing variety of Asia's many cuisines. There are formal restaurants galore, but what you are looking for is the city's wealth of street food where visiting dignitaries bond with cabdrivers at all hours of the day.'
***Patricia Schultz, Journalist, United States,
1,000 Places to See before You Die***

Singapore

Travel Facts

Where It Is

Singapore is located 136.8 km north of the Equator at the tip of the Malay peninsula, dominating the sea lanes of the Malacca Straits. Its immediate neighbours are Malaysia and Indonesia, but both Thailand and the Philippines are only a short plane ride away, making Singapore the natural gateway to Southeast Asia.

How to Get There

By Air
Singapore's Changi airport is served by over 70 airlines providing direct flights to 160 cities in 53 countries, including most of Asia, Europe and Australasia.

By Train
From Thailand and Malaysia it is possible to enter Singapore by train. There are two services available: in style and luxury aboard the Eastern & Oriental Express or by the efficient and comfortable Malaysian Railway passenger trains.

By Road
Motorists can access Singapore by car through the Malaysian town of Johor Baru. Foreign motorists are required to pay tolls and a Vehicle Entry Permit charge on weekdays.

When to Go

As Singapore lies close to the Equator its climate is characterized by uniform temperature and pressure, high humidity and abundant rainfall. Temperatures range from a minimum of 19.4 deg. C. to a maximum of 35.8 deg. C.

The climate can be divided into two main seasons, the Northeast Monsoon and the Southwest Monsoon, separated by two relatively short intermonsoon periods.

Northeast Monsoon Season: December to early March. Northeast winds prevail with cloudy conditions and frequent afternoon showers from December to January. It is relatively drier from February till early March.

Southwest Monsoon Season: June to September. Southeast/Southwest winds and hazy periods are common during this season with scattered late morning and early afternoon showers.

Travel fact information sourced from the websites listed below and the National Environment Agency website http://app.nea.gov.sg

Find Out More

Comprehensive information for visitors can be found at the Singapore Tourism Board's website **visitsingapore.com** or for more general information go to Singapore Infomap at **www.sg**

Above: *An elegant reminder of the colonial past.*

Acknowledgements

The publisher would like to thank the following whose assistance has made this book possible:

Singapore Tourism Board, Raffles Hotel, Esplanade – Theatres on the Bay, Suntec City, Raffles City, PSA Corporation, Ministry of Sound, No.5 Emerald Hill Cocktail Bar, Ramita Saisuwan, Sanskrit Kritskom and Keith Hardy.

Photo Credits

The photographs in the book were taken by *Joakim Leroy* with the exception of the following:

Raffles Hotel: 19

Singapore Tourism Board: 54, 56, 57, 58, 59, 60, 61

Authors

Joakim Leroy is a Bangkok-based French photographer. He has worked in the Southeast Asia region for several years, travelling extensively. Working in both colour and black-and-white media, his photography focuses on people, lifestyle and travel.

Michael Spencer is a travel writer and photographer based in Bangkok. He has travelled widely in Asia, Africa and South America as a correspondent for a variety of international magazines and newspapers.